When I Found YOU, I Found Me

8 Pebbles to Maintain a Healthy Soul and Achieve Purpose

Dzana Madagu

(b/w, 8x10")

With love,
Dzana Madagu
07.09.24

Dearest Dr. Cindy Trimm,

Thank you for answering the call
Thank you for being there
Thank you for being you.

Copyright

© 2022 by **Dzana Madagu**

When I Found YOU, I Found Me: 8 Pebbles to Maintain a Healthy Soul and Achieve Purpose

Pebbles for the Soul series (b/w interior).

All rights reserved. No part of this publication may be reproduced, distributed, or transmitted in any form, or by any means, including photocopying, recording or other electronic or mechanical methods, without prior written permission from the author and publisher.

Due to the dynamic nature of the internet, any web addresses or links contained in this book may have changed since publication and may no longer be valid. The views expressed in this book are solely those of the author.

Unless otherwise stated, Bible Scriptures are taken from the New King James Version®. Copyright © 1982 by Thomas Nelson. Used by permission. All rights reserved.

Scriptures marked (KJV) are taken from the King James Version (1611, 1769, Oxford University Press, Public Domain).

Scriptures marked ESV are taken from THE HOLY BIBLE, ENGLISH STANDARD VERSION ® Copyright© 2001 by Crossway, a publishing ministry of Good News Publishers. Used by permission.

Cover design, book formatting and interior design by Dr Jacqueline N Samuels - **https://tinyurl.com/AuthorJNSamuels**

Cover illustrated image, and 8 stacked pebbles (p19) by Tammy Friel.

Cover photo licensed from Shutterstock by @DaLiu.

Interior images licensed from Canva.com.

Visit the author at: **https://dzanamadagu.com**

ISBN: **9798356425523**

https://pebblesforthesoul.com

Contents

Copyright iii
Dedication vi
Acknowledgments vii
Foreword xi
Introduction xiii
PART ONE: MY STORY 1
    Day 1: It all began with a lie 2
    Day 2: Wake up and "Be" 4
    Day 3: "Where are you?" 6
    Day 4: Stay connected 9
    Day 5: "What do you see?" 10
    Day 6: Going somewhere 11
    Day 7: Change your mind 13
    Day 8: New Day 15
PART TWO: YOUR STORY 17
A Note from Dzana 18
8 Pebbles to Maintain a Healthy Soul and Achieve Purpose ... 19
Pebble 1: Discovering Truth 20
Pebble 2: Liberation/Freedom 29
Pebble 3: Self-Awareness and Identity 36
Pebble 4: Coaching, Mentoring and Empowerment 44
Pebble 5: Purpose 54
Pebble 6: Progress 60
Pebble 7: Transformation 68
Pebble 8: Authentic Living 74

About The Author 82

Appendices 83

References 85

Dedication

I am dedicating this book first to **YOU**, LORD Jesus. You are the Firstborn over all Creation, the image of the invisible GOD, Lord of all the earth, for by You all things were created that are in heaven and on earth, visible and invisible (including this book!), whether thrones or dominions or principalities or powers. All things were created through You and *for* You. Thank You, LORD.

To you reading this, with the intention and desire to be made whole in spirit, soul, and body, and ascend to new realms of freedom, healing and understanding your purpose. God sees you and has loved you with an everlasting love. It has been His ultimate desire for you to discover who you are and why you are here on earth. He longs to empower you and help you on your journey to living an authentic life of purpose and freedom to be ***you***, as you were originally designed to be! I am living proof that God's grace is available, and it is sufficient to enable wholeness and prosperity in spirit, soul and body.

It is an honour to share my story with you and some practical strategies that have blessed my personal growth. The journey continues to unfold as we are being led in victory.

Gratefully,

Dzana Madagu

https://pebblesforthesoul.com

Black & White ISBN: 9798356425523

https://dzanamadagu.com

Acknowledgments

Many people have impacted my life on various levels. Whilst it is impossible to mention everyone here, I wish to acknowledge each of the following who have had a significant input at various stages of my personal, professional and spiritual growth.

To my Mummy, Dr Mercy Jummai Sokomba, my gratitude knows no bounds. You have lovingly mentored, guided, and supported me from birth. I bless the womb from which I came. You sacrificed so much for your own children and the additional sons and daughters in the LORD who also call you 'Mummy'. Your life is an example of determination, courage and resilience. Your continuous intercession to see the purposes of God manifest in and through us is truly appreciated.

My deepest gratitude to my amazing inspirational Daddy, Professor Elijah Ndajiya Sokomba, for being there for us all, encouraging and guiding us as we each navigate our paths to divine destiny.

To my grandparents and great grandparents whom I have been so privileged to enjoy life with, may your legacies in Christ continue to touch hearts. Great Grandpa Daniel Sokomba's decision to follow the LORD and Grandpa Samson's passion for writing continue to influence my progress. I thank God for my grandmothers' love for us and their prayerful exemplary lives.

To my husband, Emmanuel aka Love of My Life and Priest of our home, I couldn't have been blessed with a more loving companion. Despite our 'healthy debates' you and I are submitted to the Lord and that continues to make a world of difference! Before we ever met, The Lord told you "*I will be like a fruitful vine in the very heart of your house*" - and so has it been, to His glory. Thank you for your loving support, making my cup of tea, and more. Marriage works! To our A-mazing boys Adriel and Azariah, you are my priceless treasures. Such an unending delight to see you both grow in wisdom, favour, and witness you both call on Jesus at your early ages. Thank you for being patient with 'busy' Mummy and giving those surprise hugs to keep me going!

To my siblings, Mary Oloyede, Ndawusa Sokomba and Paul Sokomba: I continually thank God for the privilege to grow up with you all, learning to live, love, laugh and care for each other. You all rock! Thank you. I am so blessed to have wonderful brother and sister in-laws: Oye Oloyede, Tayo Sokomba and Christine Sokomba and my precious nephews and nieces – Imisi, Tehillah, Ileri, Alyssa, Micah and Isaac.

To my beloved in-laws: Veronica Smith, Gerald Madagu, and Dafe Kokori, it is such a JOY to have you all for life. Thank you for your love.

To my mentors whom I cherish dearly:

Dr Cindy Trimm: For over two decades, you have mentored me on my journey to wholeness and purpose. I took onboard the counsel you imparted to me during our meeting regarding specific destiny paths I should take to reclaim my soul. This book is proof of my obedience: thank you.

Apostle Joshua Selman: For your encouragement, praying with me and releasing the grace to finish this book, I am grateful and honour the grace of God upon your life.

Michael AC Maynard: You were at the beginning of this book's journey. Thank you for your support, clarity and direction. The LORD orchestrated our paths to cross.

John and Pearl Osa: Thank you for always believing in my family. Your generosity in sharing your valuable time, deep spiritual wisdom, powerful intercessory secrets and more are much appreciated. Blessings and love to you!

Pastor Marjorie Esomowei and the Power Base Prophetic Intercessors Platform: Thank you all for your great mentorship in my prayer life and spiritual growth.

Dr Jacqueline N Samuels: Meeting you was part of my destiny; the confirmations we have received continually reflect this. *Like Jochebed, I have obeyed and released my 'Moses in the basket' for purpose and destiny.* Thank you for your support in publishing this book and for your prophetic midwifery services!

Thank you all for releasing the grace you have been given to invest your love, counsel, and precious time to share secrets of Kingdom success with me. I say, *"See what The LORD has done through your support and guidance"*. May His blessing continue to rest on you all.

To the great men and women of God, leading and touching lives globally through your Churches: Thank you for your encouragement, support and journeying with my family! I am blessed to follow those who through faith and patience inherit the promises.

My aunties and uncles, especially Dr Rachel Jumai Ewu, Sarah Tebu, Ladi Franklin, Comfort Audu, Lami Nathan, Elizabeth Tugba, Ore Esedebe, Jeremiah Sokomba, Moses Tsado, Dr Grace Manasoko Daniyan, Dr Godwin Ewu, and my fabulous cousins. You have all watched me grow, even as you continue to inspire and encourage me to be who I am. I sincerely acknowledge your positive impact in my life.

My childhood friends, adulthood friends and family friends, I ask the rhetorical question: *"What would life be like if I was not privileged to know you all?"* I thank you for the numerous roles you have played in polishing the brilliance of God's treasure in me. You are all part of my journey and testimony.

Rev Akila Yusuf, you are a shining example of seeding your faith through prayer, determination and action, producing lasting impact, all from humble beginnings.

To Pastor Dave & Hazel Weston, Richard & Diane Kinning, and Living Grace Church: I am so blessed to do *life* with you all and to be connected in Christ – we are family!

I am grateful to all who have prayed, encouraged me, and generously contributed towards making resources available for references.

THANK YOU ALL!

Dzana Madagu

Perseverance, persistence, focus, prayers, tears, sheer confidence in God, love for Him and the commitment to reach out to people have driven you all the years of this book's project. Many more to come, our dearest daughter.

Love, Mum and Dad

Foreword

I met Dzana for the first time at a Christian gift shop. She was looking for a unique gift for her Dad's birthday. The moment she walked in, the first thing I noticed was her smile. Sixteen (16) years later it has been a joy and honour to be married to this beautiful lady and fruitful vine. I call her my wife of many dimensions!

Over the years Dzana's faith in God has grown and this has helped her build and maintain relationships with people around her. I am constantly wowed with her ability to communicate with people at all levels.

Dzana has continued to develop her many gifts, talents and skills which include creativity, active listening, problem solving and empathy. These have helped her to effectively communicate and relate with people from diverse cultural backgrounds, provide spiritual and mentoring solutions, especially to people at crossroads in life.

As a Coach she has helped motivate and provide guidance to many people, helping them believe in themselves, achieve their goals and keep them on the path to lasting transformation. The author encourages others through her positive outlook and skilled approach to handling storms of life.

Dzana has invested time putting together the nuggets in this book that would provide light on your path to an authentic lifestyle. I recommend this book to help with soul healing and achieving your purpose in life.

Well done my Sweets!

Emmanuel Madagu

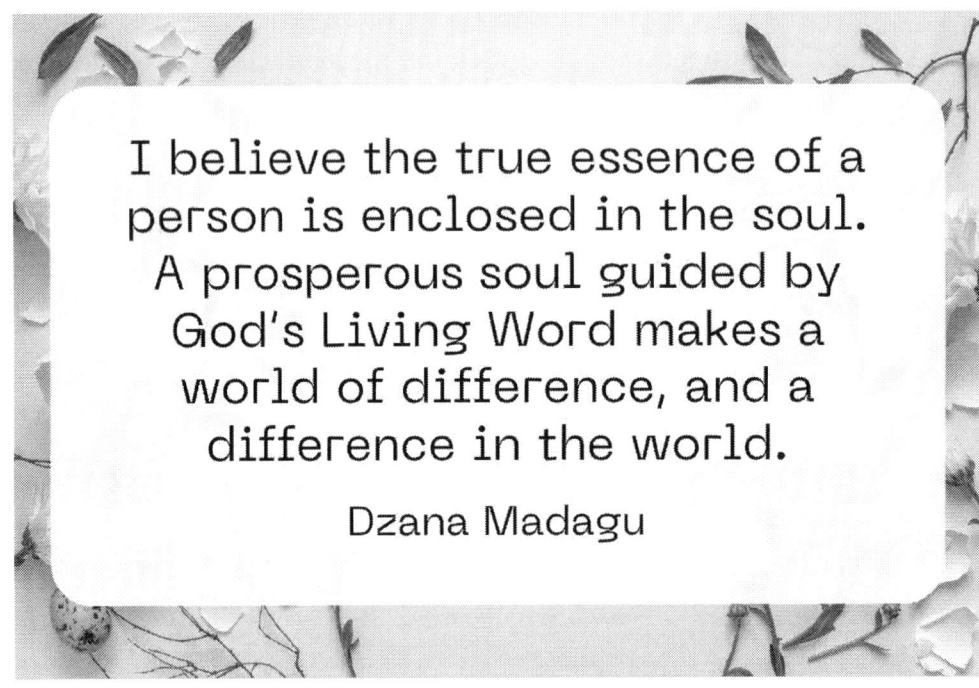

Embrace these 8 pebbles to maintain a healthy soul and achieve your purpose.

Introduction

> Knowing God helps
> you know yourself.
>
> Rick Warren

It is my deepest desire to help people discover their true identity, divine purpose, receive inner healing from past or present hurts and navigate through life with divine direction.

This book is made up of 2 Parts:

Part 1: My Story *When I Found YOU, I Found Me* – my personal experience, challenges with soul issues, and how I have been able to overcome with help from God's Word, His wisdom and divine guidance.

Part 2: Your Story *8 Pebbles to Maintain a Healthy Soul and Achieve Purpose*.

In Part 2, I work with you to guide you through soul issues, identity and empowerment and provide practical strategies, ideas and tools to help you (re)connect to God in order to live purposefully and authentically.

Life is a journey with experiences along the way (I love the canvas photo image '*Misty Road*' by Michael Busselle. It hangs beautifully in my lounge!) Whether we are aware of it or not, it does go on. Life brings situations, encounters, and series of events which we all experience at one time or the other. '*When I Found YOU, I Found Me*' is my gift to the world to bring the Light of hope, healing, meaning, understanding, direction and fresh inspiration for daily living; hence chapters are written as 'days'. '*8 Pebbles to Maintain a Healthy Soul and Achieve Purpose*' is the *travel companion* to '*When I Found YOU, I Found Me*', designed to guide you through your journey of becoming all you have been destined to be.

Note: Each pebble (stage) in Part 2 corresponds with each day in Part 1. To get the best out of your journey through this book, it is suggested that you refer to Part 1 when completing Part 2. (Feel free to colour the images).

> There is no greater agony than bearing an untold story inside you.
>
> Maya Angelou

PART ONE: MY STORY

When I found YOU, I Found Me

'With Soul Healing Comes Soul Purpose'

Pebbles for the Soul ©

By Dzana Madagu

Day 1: It all began with a lie

And you shall know the truth and the truth shall make you free. (John 8:32)

For as long as I can remember, I had always lived with a distorted image about who I really was. The faulty, untrue image had been imprinted in my soul, so I lived, perceived, and unconsciously made a lot of decisions based on faulty, erroneous perceptions. One of the major lies I held on to was that I needed to hide who I was, and I should be ashamed of myself. Foolishly, I went about life and relationships 'apologising for my existence'. It seemed the right thing to do especially as it made me feel 'humble'. Yet every now and then, there was a knowing deep within me that divine greatness and glory were seeking to find expression on the outside. Divine purpose would come knocking at my door, but I was unaware...little did I know the enemy of my soul was behind it all. To make matters worse, I *chose* to believe the lie. How can what God so fearfully and wonderfully created not be good?

It was only a matter of time that the fruit of poor choices and decisions began to ripen...and fall. A distorted image imprinted in the soul is a very dangerous weapon in the enemy's hands. When you believe in a lie and focus on it long enough, as with *whatever* you set your mind on, it becomes magnified and empowered to exist - with your permission. You set the course of your life in the direction of what you say to yourself (and believe). Your world is formed by your words.

By the mercy and goodness of God, I began to have seasons where I would pause and think deeply. It all seemed contradictory, what the Bible was saying about who I was in Christ and what I was believing about me. Something was just not quite right. With divine help, *I changed my mind* - one of the best 'unfaulty' decisions I would ever make. Thus began the battle for a daily renewed mind. I had to be intentional and desirous of true freedom. Aligning my heart and soul (and words) with The Truth of God's life-giving Word, being open to guidance and seasoned mentorship began the inner healing and ongoing journey of transformation I am eternally grateful for.

Today He (Jesus) stands at the door of your heart and knocks...He is still in the business of healing the soul and changing lives for good. If you reach out to Him with all of you, He will embrace you. Every lie will give way to Truth.

Reflection and Practical Steps:

Refer to Part 2 Your Story: *8 Pebbles to Maintain a Healthy Soul and Achieve Purpose* and complete Pebble 1: Discovering Truth

Day 2: Wake up and "Be"

Then God blessed them, and God said to them: "Be fruitful…" (Genesis 1:28)

That's it. That is all we need to do. Straight to the point. No "what ifs" or" buts". Just *"be"*. If only it were that easy. If our Creator made us be-ings, then why couldn't I just wake up and "be"? Surely there must be a missing link somewhere between the waking up and be-ing bit. The only answer I could find was to dare to ask in prayer (*ask and you shall receive*). I realised my true essence would not be revealed just like that. The blessing of being raised in a God-fearing home had its benefits but the journey to true freedom and self-discovery also required my personal input. And I lacked courage. There was fear. I did not have a clue where to begin. I doubted whether it was a good idea to find out *more* about me - as if there was not enough 'bad stuff' already that I needed to forget. I had also been harbouring soul wounds from past hurts and disappointments that weighed me down.

I dared to take the bold step to find out about my be-ing when I had *had* enough of people around me defining me based on their personal opinions, level of so-called intelligence, even greed - to use and abuse. That is what happens when you don't know what to do with what you've got, or in this case who you are!

To my pleasant surprise, snippets of me – gifts and talents (encouraging, liberating and amazing) began to show up in answer to prayer. I made the life-changing decision to be authentic and embrace balanced teaching on spiritual truths even as I began to acknowledge (and finally believe) the humbling realisation that I was created to bear fruit after all*. The Most High God designed me to bring glory through my uniqueness, talents and essence - in short, through my be-ing.

I have been saying these declarations out loud. Today I am sharing them with you to empower your positive self-awareness through the power of your intentional words:

YOU are truly one of a kind.

YOU matter.

YOU have purpose.

YOU deserve to be YOU.

YOU deserve to be heard – and seen.

God describes you as *a city that is set on a hill (which) cannot be hidden* (Matthew 5:14). Don't fret about the 'bad stuff'; just hand it all to Him for a deep clean.

I speak to you reading this, needing to hear these words: Wake up, arise, shine, be free and be fruitful in your purpose.

*See Day 6: Going Somewhere

Reflection and Practical Steps:

Refer to Part 2 Your Story: *8 Pebbles to Maintain a Healthy Soul and Achieve Purpose* and complete Pebble 2: Liberation/Freedom

Day 3: "Where are you?"

Then The LORD God called to Adam and said to him: "Where are you?"

(Genesis 3:9)

"Where are you?" The question kept echoing in my heart. I knew I was not meant to be where I was. Even more worrying, *I knew I was not where I was meant to be*. Thirsty for affirmation and validation, I decided to choose my connections or relationships on levels that would grant unrestricted access to my personal power and space. Those connections and associations became pipes that drained, sapped and stole from me. The genuine desire to relate became poisoned with ignorance, lack of proper consultation with Father God and the enemy's contribution (dangerous mix!)

Jesus comes to give us abundant life to enjoy. The enemy of our souls comes looking for us to kill, steal and destroy our lives - John10:10. He knows he just can't cause destruction unless there are legal grounds for this. When we metaphorically 'distribute' our essence through various unhealthy connections, associations and soul ties, this results in legally binding contracts in the spirit realm (very deep matters). They create grounds and inroads for the enemy to cause untold havoc in our lives.

It's all about healthy connections. Your soul needs healthy connections and relationships to thrive. With healthy connections, you refresh and get refreshed, period. We are made in God's image, after His likeness, and He desires healthy relationships too. In the cool of the day, He went searching for Adam and Eve to spend time of refreshing with them as usual…but something had gone awry. He then asked Adam: *"Where are you*?" The-One-Who-Knows-It-All was not asking the question to find out where Adam was, He was asking if Adam knew where he (Adam) was.

As fragmented as I had gradually become, I could hear the question. That is how deep The Father's love is, calling us and reaching to wherever we are, to help us out. The miraculous rescue happened when I chose to surrender my life (and mean it this time). My Prince (Jesus) came and did the 'gathering of me' from 'where I should *not be'* to 'where I *should be',* giving me His peace, His grace, His hope and a transformed identity. This is an ongoing journey.

There is joy in restoration to the original purpose written in His Book about you even before you were born. To navigate your life without divine assistance will certainly lead you to a destination you most definitely would not choose to arrive at. It is time to allow Jesus to 'gather you' from where you should **NOT** be and He will lead you to where you *should* be.

Reflection and Practical Steps:

Refer to Part 2 Your Story: *8 Pebbles to Maintain a Healthy Soul and Achieve Purpose* and complete Pebble 3: Self -Awareness and Identity

What others are saying…

There was a time in my life when the challenges seemed too great and faith was lost. It's hard to put in words the amount of support, encouragement and guidance you have given me. With your unique insight, tips, techniques and 1-2-1 coaching, I have been able to make significant moves forward in my personal life and the relationships around me. You have brought me closer to God by providing clarity through His words and for that I'm truly grateful. This is truly your calling.

P Freemantle

Day 4: Stay connected

I am the vine, you are the branches… (John 15:5)

"Do not go wandering off to do your own thing", the voice echoed in my heart.

Disobedience always comes saddled with consequences. In the beginning, in the Garden of Eden, the fall was caused by this singular act. How many times have I dared to push the boundaries and ended up in that state of *I-am-sorry-Lord-I-should have-known-better*?

The analogy of the vine and the branches in today's verse made it quite plain to see that by going it alone, I was nothing but an unfruitful plant. Yet ignorantly I perceived that since I had been redeemed, I could continually bear 'good fruit' by my own strength and wisdom. I had never been so far from the truth - literally.

Jesus makes it clear what I am and what He is. By staying connected to Him, the True Vine, I am guaranteed enduring fruitfulness. By divine design, my life is to be fruitful (produce results, good success, etc) to God's glory. Ignorance, selfishness and pride were some of the culprits that encouraged my disobedience. Instead of acknowledging the truth about my inability to consistently live supernaturally, I just kept hoping things would one day turn out right and I would be free from the cycle of highs and lows.

Until I finally came to accept the truth that my life is not my own.

All of me was bought with a price (the precious blood of Jesus) and the beauty of it is that I have been purchased from slavery into freedom and from unfruitful works into fruitfulness roundabout.

What you may count as fruitfulness through self-effort and other seemingly 'positive' means does not produce lasting results. It is only a matter of time for this truth to surface. Unless you are connected to the True Vine, Jesus Christ, your life will be devoid of fulfilling your true legacy.

After this life is through, what fruit would you have enriched humanity with? Your soul purpose matters. Today, decide to stay connected to the True Vine.

Reflection and Practical Steps:

Refer to Part 2 Your Story: *8 Pebbles to Maintain a Healthy Soul and Achieve Purpose* and complete Pebble 4: Coaching, Mentoring and Empowerment

Day 5: "What do you see?"

Then Lord answered me and said, "Write the vision, and make it plain..."
(Habakkuk 2:2)

I realised that writing down my thoughts and ideas is very much a spiritual activity as it is a physical one. The spiritual precedes the physical so writing down what I see and hear in my spirit is key to bringing the invisible into the visible. My question was, "*How would I know if what I saw and heard were in line with God's Word*?" I began to write it down anyway.

As I continued to journal my thoughts and ideas, it became apparent that some of them were planted in my heart through God's Word in seed form. I also began to recognise the ones that were not in line with God's heart towards me.

Intimacy with God through communion with His Holy Spirit brings clarity, focus and direction for life. In addition to these, He is able to infuse His Word as seed into your 'spirit man' that needs to grow. Your mind becomes renewed and transformed as you continue to feed (and feast) on His Word. To increasingly delight yourself in spending quality time with Him means you will begin to see life from a higher perspective - His perspective. In short, He reveals the mystery of His Word to you through His Spirit.

God does not operate the way man does so He is always willing to show you how to get good success in life. Everything you need to succeed has been 'embedded in you'. At the right time and season, He inspires you through divine thoughts, ideas and direction on how to bring out what **HE** put inside of you. He instructs you to write what you see as plainly as possible, so you can focus, gain clarity, ask for and receive revelation knowledge, guidance and the necessary support to achieve your vision and ultimately, purpose.

Do you know that ***tangible realities are attracted to vision written down***? A divinely inspired vision attracts Heaven's resources or **PROVISION** to fulfil its mandate.

What is your vision? What do you see?

Reflection and Practical Steps:

Refer to Part 2 Your Story: *8 Pebbles to Maintain a Healthy Soul and Achieve Purpose* and complete Pebble 5: Purpose

Day 6: Going somewhere

And God is able to make all grace (every favour and earthly blessing) come in abundance to you… (2 Corinthians 9:8 AMP)

When I discovered the liberating TRUTH that what Jesus came to do for me meant I could switch from the status of being fearful and unfruitful to the preferred status of a life filled with great achievements, impact and purpose, this opened me up to a realm of possibilities. Those divine imaginations, passions and aspirations which I experienced from childhood began to resurface on a whole new level. So God has been with me all along? I mused. *Of course - He was there in the beginning!* It became apparent that I had all the resources necessary to carry out my God-given *mission-now-possible.* What a privilege!

There was one thing though…how do I go about it? (*Crickets chirping…lol*)

As excited as I was to intentionally begin to live fruitfully*, I also needed to grow in my understanding of God's standards. At first, it felt very restrictive in a negative sense to be honest, because I thought I would have to work hard to live by endless (unbroken) rules. By the way, these 'rules' are designed for our own good (1 John 5:3).

When God set His standards, He did not look at your ability to meet up with them. Man can never attain God's standards for living a successful life. He looked at *His* ability through the person of Jesus and presence of the Holy Spirit, to empower us to enjoy a productive life in its fullness - successfully and joyfully. This is where His divine grace (aka ability) comes in, to usher and steward the specific resources needed to execute divine assignments which include living in obedience to God's standards. He promises reward for obedience, for instance see Deuteronomy 28:1.

It is necessary for you to be infused with His empowering resources through His grace for the journey ahead and the mission to accomplish. You were not designed to carry out your divine assignment on the strength of your effort and abilities alone while adhering to a long list of rules. His standards also include a life of freedom from unhealthy soul entanglements that will certainly hinder your progress.

Rest assured that God is intentional in His dealings with you. It may seem as if you are jogging on the spot, but you are going somewhere – by His grace.

Let this truth liberate your soul today.

*See Day 2: Wake up and "Be"

Reflection and Practical Steps:

Refer to Part 2 Your Story: *8 Pebbles to Maintain a Healthy Soul and Achieve Purpose* and complete Pebble 6: Progress

What others are saying…

Thank you for inspiring me, Dzana. Your words are amazing.

J Edkins

Day 7: Change your mind

...But we have the mind of Christ. (1 Corinthians 2:16, KJV)

Emotional pain, ignorance and disappointment followed me around like faithful assistants. Bruised by deception, lack of encouragement and rejection, there I was, having to muster courage to keep on moving in the divine direction set before me. My wounded soul struggled with these issues and more, for a long time. Then The Lover of my soul (Jesus) began to woo me, His bride. I heard Him speak to me, telling me I am His chosen and consecrated temple, where His eyes and heart will always be (see 2 Chronicles 7:16). It was hard to comprehend that I was still so desirable despite these unresolved weighty issues...***I needed a change of mind.***

I therefore decided to trust Him with my pain and in short, my life – past, present and future. It was then I came to realise that ONLY Jesus can love, understand so perfectly, bring grace, wisdom needed to see and live above life's circumstances. By embracing this truth (through various forms of divine assistance and proven strategies) and **deciding** to live by it, my life changed for good. My soul began to heal when I decided to view life through His perspective.

Life happens to the living. Challenging situations come our way, unfortunate unexpected events occur, trust gets broken, etc. We all respond to life in different ways depending on various factors including personality, background, knowledge, experience, upbringing and orientation. However, to live a victorious life, we need the mind of Christ - an invaluable asset to have.

With the mind of Christ, you are empowered to view life from a divine perspective. You are enabled to 'see' by divine revelation through The Holy Spirit what God had prepared in advance for you to succeed and the way out of every quagmire you may encounter. It also brings the power to influence positive change in your life and affect the lives of those around you for good. The love of God is so great that He has graciously made it possible for you to journey through life with joy, hope, victory (and fun!) irrespective of the unfortunate unexpected events, including those caused by your own shortcomings.

It takes a humble heart to acknowledge the need for the ability to **THINK** like Jesus. You will be able to align truth with what you say and what you really believe on the inside about you and your circumstances. This will help in navigating you towards countless victories, answered prayers and prosperity of your spirit, soul and body.

Reflection and Practical Steps:

Refer to Part 2 *Your Story: 8 Pebbles to Maintain a Healthy Soul and Achieve Purpose* and complete Pebble 7: Transformation

Day 8: New Day

This is the day the LORD has made… (Psalm 118:24)

I am so excited to share what this DAY looks like to me. For starters, this is The Day that I conclude the final step to my journey of finding out who I am in this book!

This is the Day that I am 'now showing' so to speak. I have woken up (and I am committed to staying 'awake' in a manner of speaking) to become unapologetic, confident, secure, reassured and in awe of God's idea that I am actually His idea. So, I *'owe no one anything, except to love...'* (Romans 13:8)

The security through divine revelation which I now experience coming from the depth of God's love and acceptance of me has settled any doubts about my significance and what treasures I have been blessed with to share with you.

"*But we have this treasure in earthen vessels, that the excellence of the power may be of God and not of us.*" (2 Corinthians 4:7)

I am who I am because He is who He is.

My success, advancement and fulfilment in this life and thereafter are not predicated on what I do but who I am in Christ - herein lies the mystery to my true identity.

For the past 7 days, I:

- Began with believing a lie
- Woke up to 'be'
- Found where I am
- Stayed connected (choices)
- Saw what I needed to see (vision)
- Started going somewhere (led by His grace)
- Changed my mind (transformation)

And on this 8th day, it's a New Day to live authentically!

The beauty of it all is that you can journey through each day (from Day 1 to 8 in this book) with whatever challenges you at your core and prayerfully trust God to help you come out whole - spirit, soul and body. This is how God led me and is still leading me in specific areas as I become more and more of what He had in mind when He created me.

It takes a willing and submissive heart, with humility, brokenness, and trust in God's way of doing life - I found the path to life, **abundant life** and I hope this helps to guide you in finding it too!

Reflection and Practical Steps:

Refer to Part 2 *Your Story: 8 Pebbles to Maintain a Healthy Soul and Achieve Purpose* and complete Pebble 8: Authentic Living.

PART TWO: YOUR STORY

You are a diamond worth honouring and celebrating. It's time to honour who you truly are and reflect your Divine calling and purpose.

Dr Jacqueline Samuels ©

A Note from Dzana

Welcome to an authentic life of purpose and freedom to be **you**, just as you were originally designed to be!

Your decision to engage on this journey is proof that you are on the right track. It wasn't until I made the decision to discover the truth about me that my world began to change in the right direction. I discovered that as life happens to us through various circumstances, we need to pay close attention to the effect it has on our souls. I needed soul healing so desperately, having experienced the effects of identity crisis, deception, fear, disappointment, despair, un-forgiveness, resentment, etc. My willingness to go on the journey to wholeness was how I also discovered my passion and desire to see others made whole in spirit, soul, and body and ascend to new realms of freedom, healing and understanding purpose.

In Part One of this book, I shared *my* story with you. This is your opportunity and space to take some time to engage with *your* story by working through the 8 *Pebbles that correspond with each day in Part One.

The pebbles have been carefully and prayerfully designed with you in mind. It contains over 25 years of experience with 'soul issues' and serves as a practical guide for discovering who you are, fulfilling your divine purpose and shows you how to maintain your soul on a daily basis. I have also included personal strategies and tips to support you as you embark on your journey.

Did you know that pebbles are stones that have been made smooth by water and sand? God's Word is likened to water. I believe all eight pebbles to achieving and maintaining a prosperous soul are made smooth by the WORD of God. Apply them to make your way prosperous so you can have good success in life.

Working through each pebble takes you from one level of growth, healing and freedom to the next. You will fully benefit by completing all eight stages.

Remember it is the *continuous* activity of water that smoothens the pebbles over time. This means it requires your consistency, determination, intentionality and **choosing daily** to allow God's WORD, by the power of the Holy Spirit, to do the work within your soul.

God's earnest desire for you is *to prosper and be in health, just as your soul prospers* (3 John 2). Be encouraged, for with God ALL things are possible.

With love and blessings,

Dzana

* **Pebbles** refer to stages

8 Pebbles to Maintain a Healthy Soul and Achieve Purpose

Pebble 1: Discovering Truth

From Day 1: It all began with a lie
- Discover and embrace Truth, discard falsehood and negative beliefs.

> Man will occasionally stumble over the truth, but most of the time he will pick himself up and continue on.
>
> Winston Churchill

Digging Deep

We live in a world where truth has been exchanged or traded for falsehood, lies, denial, fame, fortune, recognition, you name it. Unhealthy, controlling and dysfunctional relationships have also resulted in robbing us of our true essence. This is why there is so much hurt, pain, deception and disease plaguing humanity today. Every time the truth is undermined the effect creates a negative imprint on the human soul. Life becomes less authentic and slowly spirals downwards.

Truth is defined as the quality of being true. *(Cambridge Dictionary)*

Truth is also a quality used to define utterances that are from The Lord. *(Bakers Evangelical Dictionary of Biblical Theology)* Whatever God says is **truth**.

To discover the truth about who you are is a process that moves from one level to the next. Rather than pursuing truth as an occasional exercise, it should be a consistent growth process.

How does the 'truth process' take place?

It takes your willingness to 'face the music' of what is going on in your life. You get to decide to make a change in the right direction towards a life of freedom from the shackles of lies, self-defeating habits and ignorance.

You need the following attributes to pursue the truth:

- Courage
- Discipline
- Determination
- Honesty
- Humility
- Faith

Can you list 4 more? In what areas are you lacking and what will you do about them?

The truth is often resisted yet it holds the key to freedom. Once truth is embraced and accepted about any given situation, the result includes a sense of weight being lifted from the shoulders.

Reflection:

List five instances from your journey through life so far where you have resisted the truth about you (good or bad) and why you resisted.

1.

2.

3.

4.

5.

What emotions did you experience while you resisted the truth? What did you do next?

Face to Face with *You* (when you need to make a change)

Pride, arrogance, ignorance, fear of rejection, low self-esteem and shame are some examples of why we hide from or resist the truth. Today you are going to let go of every resistance and give a detailed description below of how you see yourself.

> The human heart unwilling to submit to the truth will never know the truth.
>
> CBN.com

Resource on Truth:
http://www.cbn.com/spirituallife/onlinediscipleship/easter/what_is_truth.aspx

The Truth about You (your original identity)

Negative beliefs and perceptions will always limit your ability to see beyond your present reality and this can also affect how you think. Your internal dialogue is more real than what you speak out. Your beliefs, perceptions and what you say need to be properly aligned with truth in order to make a lasting change, and for you to come to the wonderful discovery of who you were originally created to be.

To enable this alignment take place, it starts with the WORD of God (which is The Way, The Truth and The Life).

John 1:1 says: *"In the beginning was the Word and the Word was with God, and the Word was GOD".* God is His Word. He always creates whatever He does with His life-giving Word.

There is the truth about who you really are. It is liberating. This means it will set you free from lies, limiting and erroneous perceptions, fear, doubt, etc. Reconnecting with God, who is the Creator of the universe, will bring you to the amazing revelation of who you truly are.

Since you were created in God's image and likeness, your words also create your world. (See Hebrews 11:13, Psalm 33:6)

Reflect on the following:

1. What words have you been speaking over your life lately (internally and externally)?

2. What words have people, for instance loved ones, friends, associates, acquaintances, etc. and challenges spoken about you?

3. What words have you accepted into your life that have not been helpful?

The Truth about You (continued)

Jesus says:

"*You shall know the TRUTH and the TRUTH shall make you free.*" (John 8:32, emphasis mine)

You need spend time gaining knowledge of what God says. This will help you to put a stop to the influx of negative words and uproot beliefs that do not bring life, health and wholeness to your soul (mind, will and emotions). Choose to allow what God says about you to take the driver's seat in your life.

You need to **choose** to do this daily: As soon as you wake up, before you begin your day, choose to embrace the truth of who God says you are. In time, you will see the fruit of choosing to align with God's unfailing Word (remember the pebble is made smooth by the *continuous* activity of water overtime).

Here are some daily decisions that have helped me. You can use them as a guide for daily declarations and take some time to write out yours.

I choose to live in truth

I am who God says I am, and I **choose** to believe Him

I am God's masterpiece

I will live to declare God's goodness in my life

I am forgiven

I am destined for greatness

I am favoured

Be creative. Use colourful sticky notes on the fridge, bathroom mirror, car dashboard, behind your front door. Whenever you sight them, read them out. Set the declarations as reminders on your phone, tablet, etc.

Embracing Truth

And you shall know the truth, and the truth shall make you free.

(John 8:32)

Take some time to look at your schedule and priorities.

1. What does your calendar look like?

2. What activities and positive habits can you engage in that would help you to allow the Light of God's Word to gain entrance into your soul, and continually bring the TRUTH?

Declaration of Commitment

In your own words, write a paragraph of your own personalised declaration of commitment to the strategies you will adopt to give continuous access to the truth of God's Word into your soul.

Pebble 2: Liberation/Freedom

From Day 2: Wake Up and 'Be'
- Live out your true self, soul healing, confidence.

We know through painful experience that freedom is never voluntarily given by the oppressor; it must be demanded by the oppressed.

Martin Luther King Jr.

What does 'Freedom' look like?

In Pebble 1, we explored truth based on God's Word and how this truth sets us free. This next step titled Liberation/Freedom (also known as Deliverance) refers to being given the keys (access) into a delightful garden (Eden) – a life of possibilities, abundance and purpose.

Here are a couple of definitions of **freedom** from the Cambridge dictionary:

"The condition or right of being able or allowed to do, say, think, etc. whatever you want to, without being controlled or limited."

"The state of not being in prison or in the condition of slavery."

From a biblical perspective, I have adjusted the first definition: "The condition or right of being able or allowed to do, say, think and BE who God has called you to be and fully equipped with all you need to succeed in line with His purpose."

I personally believe this is the ultimate and truest freedom a person can experience.

Action:

Close your eyes for a couple of minutes. Think about the word FREEDOM. What images come to your mind? Describe them briefly below.

Beyond the Veil

Ignorance and fear can cast a veil (or mask) over your understanding of who you are. However, when you turn to The Lord Jesus, the veil is taken away.

"Nevertheless when it shall turn to the Lord, the vail shall be taken away.17 Now the Lord is that Spirit: and where the Spirit of the Lord is, there is liberty." (2 Corinthians 3:16-17, KJV).

Liberty therefore gives you:

- Freedom to be YOU (as God originally intended)
- Freedom to GROW in knowledge and understanding
- Freedom from the FEAR of people's opinion about you
- Freedom from demonic OPPRESSION

Action:

List other areas in your life where freedom needs to reign

Soul Wounds

Life is full of ups and downs as the popular saying goes. The problem is the 'downs' we all face have a way of affecting us at the soul level, resulting in emotional scars which keep us in bondage.

These scars remain sensitive, and the slightest trigger event can cause us to react, further reinforcing the soul wound(s). Your soul is the essence of who you are.

The soul is us at our core, what makes everyone unique.

Soul wounds can occur from:

- Rejection
- Abuse
- Humiliation
- Injustice
- Betrayal, etc.

These could result in bitterness, resentment, un-forgiveness, low self-esteem, and others.

Action:

Look back at how life has been and where you may have fallen victim to the situations listed above - or similar ones. Can you identify at least 5 soul wounds you are yet to be healed from? List them below.

The Way Forward

Points to note:

- If you have discovered wounds within your soul, healing and freedom are prerequisites to moving forward in life.
- Soul wounds will affect how you see yourself and place limits on your capabilities.
- God is able to bring true, lasting healing through His Word, by the power of His Spirit.
- Soul healing is a process and can take some time.
- Seeking godly, practical support through prayer, balanced spiritual mentorship, counselling (especially from a balanced and sound biblical perspective) or speaking to a mature born-again Christian in confidence are some of the practical ways you can get help.

Action:

Pause. Pray. Decide to move forward.

What other practical ways can you identify and commit to, that will help you on your journey to soul healing?

God Loves You

Reflect on the above heading.

God wants to give you BOLDNESS, CONFIDENCE and everything you need to succeed in life.

God's unending love for you and commitment to have a lasting love relationship with you is the reason He came to earth as the Man Jesus, to die so you can live a glorious, fulfilled and abundant life in total wholeness.

It is His uppermost desire for you to prosper and be in good health "*even as your soul prospers*" (3 John 2).

By connecting with the above truths, your true essence can find true expression. God, your Creator, will readily introduce you to YOU by the power of His Spirit.

You can wake up from all that has held you back and BE who you are.

Prayer:

Have you made a commitment to follow Jesus? If not, I encourage you to take a moment to declare the following prayer and invite Him into your heart. The LORD Jesus is inviting you into His Kingdom of Light and Love today. He comes into your heart by invitation only.

Sinner's prayer.

LORD Jesus, I acknowledge that You died for my sins. I am a sinner. Today I ask You to wash away all my sins and make me new. I want to grow in Your love and grace as You lead and guide me every day. Thank You, LORD, for saving me and giving me a new life and heart, in the Name of Jesus. Amen.

Jesus says in Revelation 3:20: "*Behold, I stand at the door and knock. If anyone hears My voice and opens the door, I will come in to him and dine with him, and he with Me.*" Welcome to the family of God!

If you have sincerely prayed the above Sinners prayer and would like to enroll in 4 week course titled: ' *God's Kingdom - Navigating Your Way'* please email me for more details: dzana@pebblesforthesoul.com

Note: Page 44 (Pebble 4) has some information on how to connect and grow in the family of God.

Daily Declarations

You are unique and one of a kind. There will never be another you.

This is your space to write out 10 affirmation statements you can declare/read out loud with confidence every day for the next 21 days until they become part of your belief system. Here are some examples to get you started:

- My life is blessed and highly favoured.
- It is my legacy to thrive.
- I love what I do, and I am good at it.
- I am exactly where I need to be right now.

Your turn…

Remember: Your world is framed by your words.

Pebble 3: Self-Awareness and Identity

From Day 3: Where Are You?
- 'Gather you', making healthy connections, relationships, discovering who you are.

> The key to unlocking all you are supposed to be is in the relationships you make in life— first your relationship with God, and then your relationship with others who are in tune with Him.

Dr Cindy Trimm

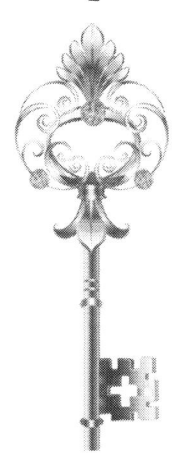

Do You Know Where You Are?

It has been said that you can only start from where you are.

The courageous steps taken in Pebbles 1 & 2 of this journey helped to shed light on areas you need to address so that you can move forward including:

- Coming to terms with the truth
- Freedom and soul healing

Action:

Write out at least 5 other areas you have identified from your personal journey through Pebbles 1 & 2 that you are currently working through:

From the above areas, what strategies will you be using to achieve progress?

Right Connections

Read the excerpt below and answer the questions that follow.

Getting Back on Course

God's solution for us is not only spiritual salvation, but also our real-time relationship with the Holy Spirit. I once heard Peter Greig teach that the Spirit of God is like one of those GPS navigational systems. We call it the *"God Positioning System."* The Holy Spirit, like our modern-day GPS when you take a wrong turn, doesn't throw up its hands and say, *"Well now you've done it! You're lost! There is no way I can help you now!"* Instead, it simply says, *"Recalculating...recalculating...."*

God considers where you are now - no matter how far off course you get - and determines a way to get you to where you were originally supposed to be. That doesn't mean there won't be some back tracking or travelling through parts of town you would prefer to avoid. However, if you follow that still small Voice of God within you, He will get you back on course to your intended destination. It won't happen overnight, but it will happen if you walk with Him step by step. There might be some retraining involved - or some self-disciplining required - but as the Bible promises:

"For the moment, all discipline seems painful rather than pleasant, but later it yields the peaceful fruit of righteousness to those who have been trained by it." (Hebrews 12:11, ESV)

Source: Dr Cindy Trimm, *'Reclaim Your Soul' Your Journey to Personal Empowerment*

1. Where have you missed your turning in terms of your relationships?

2. What toxic connections/associations/relationships will you be letting go of, with God's help?

Developing Positive Relationships

Epictetus, the Stoic Philosopher made a profound statement: *"The key is to keep company only with people who uplift you, whose presence call forth your best"*.

In keeping with the right company, you are staying true to who you are and safeguarding your identity.

Reflect on certain positive relationships in your life. How do they inspire you to be who you are?

Now, think deeply about people you are connected to that seek to control you or alter who you are.

To successfully disengage from those unhealthy connections, here are some areas that would require your attention:

- Mindset
- Habits
- Beliefs
- Core Values

Do some further research on the above areas and commit to adjusting as required.

Becoming Self-Aware

You are a unique multifaceted being.

Take a moment to pause and be quiet within you. There is an internal dialogue going on within about who you really are. As honestly as you can be, describe who you believe you are on the inside. That amazing person you wish everyone could meet.

***Action*:**

In the diamond below, write **6 areas** you are aware of that reflect your unique gifts and talents: What steps will you take to develop them further? You can also colour the diamond if you wish!

When you are Self-aware, you can see where your thoughts and emotions are guiding you. (Developinggoodhabits.com)

In addition, you can partner with God through The Holy Spirit to make necessary changes in the direction of your future (see the *Getting Back on Course* excerpt on page 39).

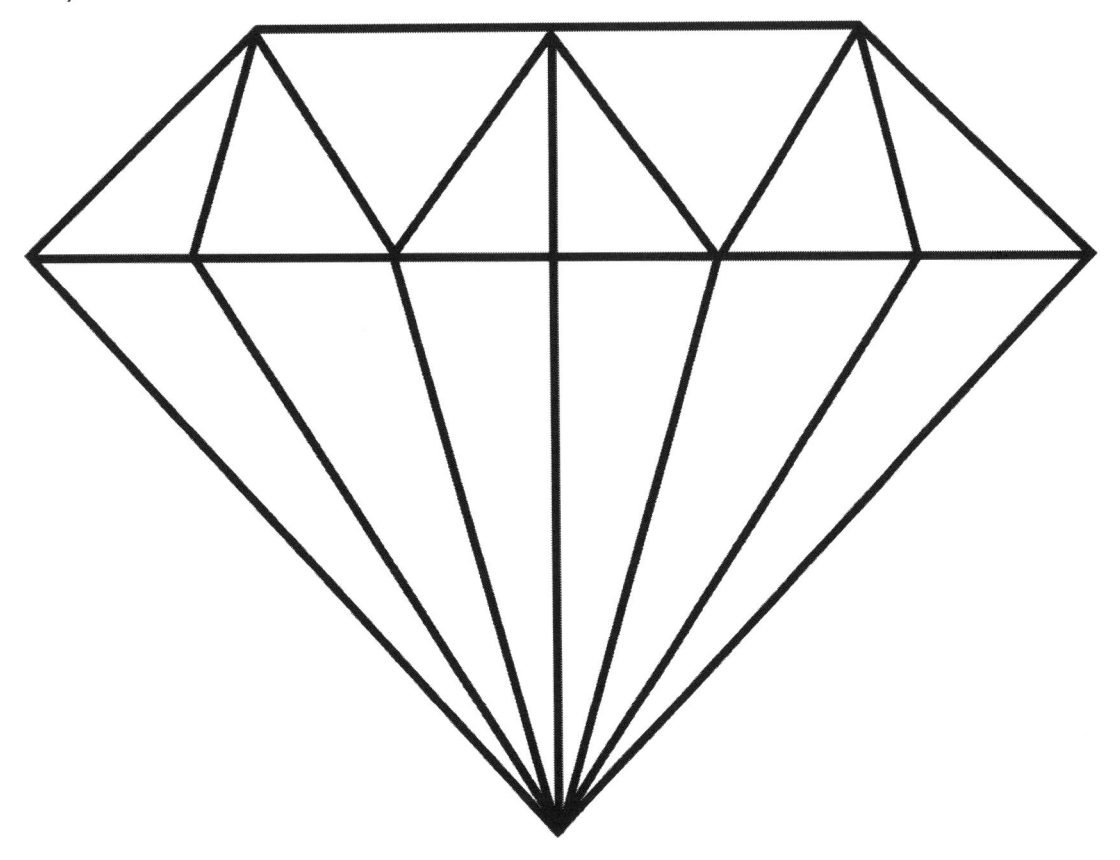

Your True Identity

In the beginning, God… (Genesis 1:1)

This is the starting point in finding your true identity. Your true self is who you are by original design, and who you are becoming. Starting with God by connecting to Him is the beginning.

Back to the story of Adam and Eve after they sinned:

They lost their **true identity**

They were fearful

They were ashamed

They were hiding

They opened the door to separation from God

Can you mention other areas that got affected by their disobedience? Read Genesis 3:1-24.

Your true identity is linked to your purpose. When you find God, then all you need to succeed in life will gravitate towards the real you. This is what the title of My Story is about – **When I found YOU (GOD), I found me (the real me).** This has only been possible with God, through His Word (Jesus) and by the Holy Spirit.

Prayer to Reconnect to God

Heavenly Father, I thank You for Your love.
I thank You for Your original desire to have a loving relationship with me,
And for choosing me to bring You glory on earth
With the wonderful gifts and talents You have given me.
I thank You for creating me as one of a kind, with a purpose,
And there can never be another me.
I ask that by Your Holy Spirit, You take me back to where I need to be,
And restore me to Your original plan before sin got in the way.
My life will then know and experience the fulfilment it has always longed for,
And I will forever share the joy of knowing YOU, finding YOU and being connected to YOU.
Thank You for every answered prayer.
In the Name of Jesus. Amen.

By Dzana Madagu

Pebble 4: Coaching, Mentoring and Empowerment

From Day 4: Stay Connected

- The blessing of mentoring accountability, guidance, and support.

What others are saying…

Dearest Dzana,
I thank God for your life and
TO GOD BE ALL THE GLORY.
I knew that there would be a day such
as this when our awesome GOD would
use you to help in impacting peace
and tranquility in the lives of troubled
people in this troubled world. The
Lord will give you His strength,
knowledge and wisdom in helping
people through your Life Coaching.
Well done dearest Dzana.
SHALOM!

Helen-Rose Ukaegbu

But grow in the grace and knowledge of our Lord and Saviour Jesus Christ. To Him be the glory both now and forever. Amen.

(2 Peter 3:18)

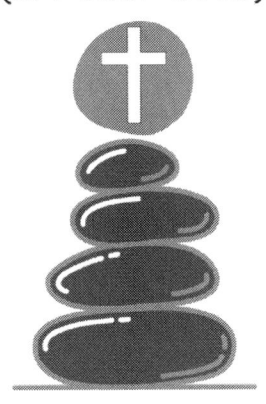

Growth and Grace

Growth is defined as the act or **process** or a manner of growing, development or gradual increase *(Dictionary.com)*.

Grace is the divine ability given to ensure growth takes place. Jesus Christ is FULL of grace and truth therefore maintaining that connection to Him secures the opportunity to grow, increase, and develop from one stage to another.

How does maintaining the connection work? This done through:

- Prayer
- Fasting
- Studying the Bible (God's Word)
- Mentoring
- Reading books authored by seasoned individuals
- Attending training courses – online and face to face
- Attending teaching sessions, conferences, seminars and workshops
- Connecting with like-minded believers
- Having God centred relationships
- Using your gifts and talents to serve
- Giving (sacrificial giving – using your finances, time, skills, resources)
- Strategic networking

Action:

List 5 areas that can further support your growth:

How can you tell if you are growing?

Connected to Grow

Plants need water, nutrients and proper environmental conditions in order to grow. The same goes for you and me - we need to be watered by God's Word, nourished with balanced teaching, and challenged through coaching/mentoring to succeed.

Jesus gives insight using the analogy of the vine and branches to introduce the concept of mentoring – so you can bear fruit (see John 15:1-8). Remember Pebble 2 takes you through God's original plan for mankind to be fruitful.

Action:

Describe 3 areas in your life where you have identified growth.

Now list three areas where you are yet to see growth:

Without the right support, growth is limited or even frustrated. As much as you may prefer to go it alone or do your own thing, it is only a matter of time before frustration sets in.

Pebbles For The Soul ©

The Benefits of Coaching and Mentoring

Coaching provides training and support to help a person prepare for something.

Mentoring is essentially about helping a person develop more effectively.

A great mentor:

- Is a subject matter expert
- He or she focuses on development, not performance
- Challenges you to grow
- Maintains relationship integrity
- Is a patient guide
- Points out potential obstacles through insight
- Keeps you on track with your purpose
- Is humble

Action:

List 8 areas in your life that would benefit from coaching or being mentored:

If you are serious about growth, prayerfully ask God to lead you to the right mentor either online or face to face to support you in achieving your purpose.

Paying attention to the areas listed below will help you to grow in grace and bear fruit. Can you describe what each word means to you?

Accountability

Commitment

Personal development

Character

Habits

Action:

List 5 action points you commit to follow through to help you locate the right coach/mentor.

Empowered by The Holy Spirit

To empower someone means to give them the means to achieve something, for example, to become stronger or more successful *(Collins Dictionary)*.

"Behold, I send the Promise of my Father upon you: but tarry in the city of Jerusalem until you are endued with power from on high." (Luke 24:49)

The Holy Spirit is the greatest Empowerment Specialist. When you are empowered by The Holy Spirit, you can effectively function in your divine purpose. This does not mean you should not take the initiative to hone your skills or improve on yourself.

Another key thing to note - when you are yielded to The Holy Spirit, He is able to:

- Align you with the right connections in every season relevant to your purpose
- Inspire you to take certain timely steps that will lead you to doors of opportunities and favour
- Give you clarity and understanding on how to develop your gifts with specific resources to invest your time in – like books, teachings (online or offline) training sessions, live events etc. so you can focus your time and energy on where you need to be, and what you need to be doing at specific seasons to nurture your purpose
- Give you the boldness and wisdom to say "No" to activities which will take you off track thus enabling you to say "Yes" to activities that will keep you on track
- Teach you how to market your personal brand (He can divinely inspire you by leading you to someone who knows how to help you in this area)
- Help you identify your seasons to take breaks, REST and get refreshed (with no apologies!)

Below is one of my favourite Bible verses for direction; it has been a guiding light in major decision making:

"Your ears shall hear a word behind you saying, "This is the way, walk in it", whenever you turn to the right hand or whenever you turn to the left." (Isaiah 30:21)

Can you think of times where help came your way, but you rejected it based on fear, self-consciousness, pride, ignorance, procrastination, laziness or some other reason? Give two instances.

1.

2.

Declaration of Commitment

I will prayerfully locate a coach or mentor who is spiritually mature, with proven track record(s) of positive results and who can help me in developing my purpose.

I will begin by…

Suggested resources for further equipping:

John Maxwell: *15 Laws of Growth*

James Clear: *Atomic Habits*

Dr Jacqueline N Samuels: *Push Through: Release Your Past and Step into Your Divine Destiny*

Investors in People.com

Mind Tools.com

Pebble 5: Purpose

From Day 5: What Do You See?

- The power of vision, knowing why you exist, where you belong.

> But as it is written: "Eye has not seen, nor ear heard, nor have entered into the heart of man the things which God has prepared for those who love Him." But God has revealed them to us through His Spirit. For the Spirit searches all things, yes, the deep things of God.
>
> (1 Corinthians 2:9-10)

Clarity

Clarity is defined as *the quality of being clear and easy to understand, see or hear.* (Cambridge dictionary). For instance, sharpness of image or clarity of sound.

Words related to clarity include:

- Accuracy
- Exactness
- Precision

And he looked up and said, "*I see men like trees walking.*" Then He put His hands on his eyes again and made him look up. And he was restored and saw everyone clearly. (Mark 8: 24-25)

In the above Bible passage, the full account relates to where Jesus heals a blind man. The healing miracle was done in two phases. In the first phase, the blind man could see but not clearly. In the second phase, he saw everyone clearly.

Action:

Why is clarity an important element in understanding your vision?

Writing Your Vision

"Vision is not something you conjure up in your own imagination, but through prayerful consideration you discern the will of God for your life (Job 32:8). Once you have your vision, you can then discipline yourself to write the vision down and put feet to what you have written." (From Dr Cindy Trimm, *'Hello, TOMORROW!' The Transformational Power of Vision*)

The process of writing your vision is not to be rushed. It calls for careful and prayerful periods of being open to listening for Divine guidance.

Action:

Do you already have a vision for your life/future?

If yes, what does it look like?

What tools/resources do you have to enable you sharpen your vision?

Creating Your Vision Board (Practical exercise)

This begins with your state of mind. Free your mind from clutter like past hurts, negative thinking, fear, unbelief, self-limitation, doubts, etc. The first 4 Pebbles will help to address these areas and more, to prepare you for this practical exercise.

Next, envision your future by taking a few moments to harness the power of your imagination and begin to think about the quality of life you desire to live.

Allow your mind to capture images that you can find in magazines, on the internet, or elsewhere, to help with creating your vision board.

Items you will need include markers, post-it notes, pictures/photos, a corkboard/noticeboard or large cardboard, glue, blue tack - whatever will help to illustrate your ideas!

The whole idea is for you to have your future in front of your eyes, clarify what is most important to you and remove distractions that will take you off track in achieving your goals. Include positive and motivational words, quotes or affirmations. Be as creative as you can be (there is no scoring or award marks for vision boards!).

Action:

Your vision board is an ongoing work in progress so be flexible and willing to update it as required. Remember, you are always evolving to superior versions of who you are. What would your dream life look like?

Go ahead and create! You can come back and add to your vision board as you evolve. Remember to hang it where you can see it every day!

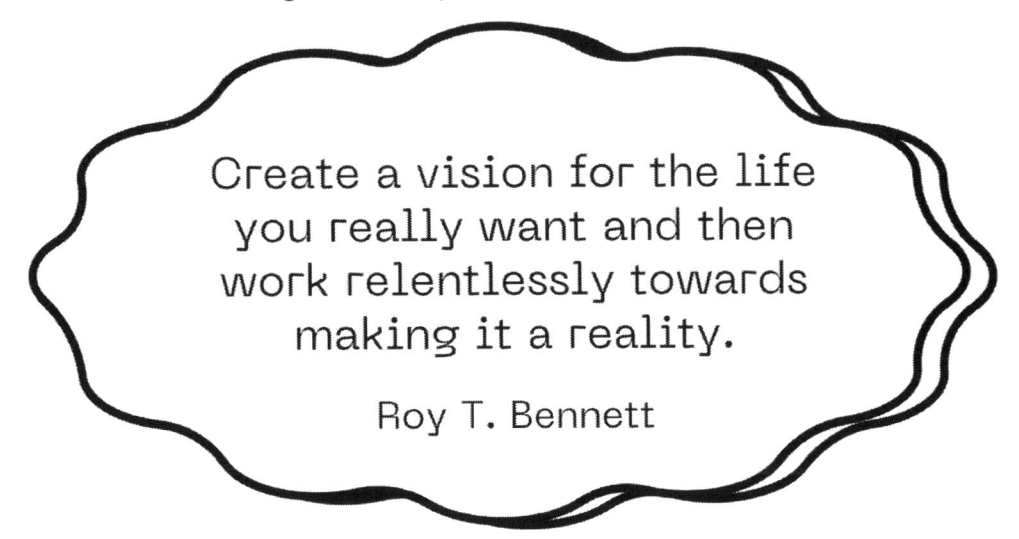

> Create a vision for the life you really want and then work relentlessly towards making it a reality.
>
> Roy T. Bennett

Understanding Your Purpose

This is key to your empowerment. It is crucial to know who you are, why you are here, your values, beliefs, gifts and talents. Knowing these will save you untold heartache and rescue you from cycles of being a 'square peg in a round hole'. Understanding your purpose will empower you to:

- Invest your time with wisdom by saying *yes* to the right activities
- Focus on those skills that will improve your chances of success in life
- Save you from the trap of competing with others
- Stay on your own life's lane (focus)
- Envying successes of others (instead, you celebrate their achievements)

Refer to a time in your life when you understood a certain role/task and you had the necessary skills, tools and support to perform your responsibility. How did it make you feel?

Understanding your purpose helps to demystify life.

Can you comment on the above statement?

Tip:

Taking assessments and personality tests are some of the ways to help you gain deeper insight to who you are. Some trusted websites to take these include: Myers-Briggs.org, DiscProfile.com, High5Test.com.

Declaration of Commitment:

Heavenly Father, I commit to spending time with You and listening to Your Holy Spirit, for only then will I be able to hear, see clearly and write down the vision You have given for my life.

> Then the Lord answered me and said: "Write the vision and make it plain on tablets, that he may run who reads it."
>
> (Habakkuk 2:2-3)

Pebble 6: Progress

From Day 6: Going Somewhere
- Moving forward, spiritual progress, LIGHT.

They go from strength to strength, each one appears before God in Zion.
(Psalm 84:7)

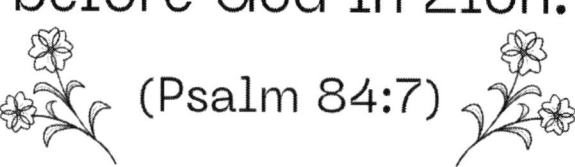

Moving On (Part 1)

As you already know, receiving the gift of salvation is the beginning of a lifelong journey into your divine purpose.

It is by grace we are saved through faith in Jesus, and not by works so no one can boast. There are also other ways God in His goodness extends the grace you need to actively engage with to help you fulfil our purpose.

*Some of the ways include:

1. Mentoring and support from the five-fold ministry in the Church (Apostles, Prophets, Teachers, Evangelists and Pastors) and connecting with like-minded Christians.

Connecting to a Church that embraces the full gospel of the Kingdom. It should also be enriched with sound biblical doctrines and teachings, seminars, conferences and activities that will encourage spiritual progress, personal development, character building, accountability, etc.

Are you connected to a Spirit-filled Church (a Church guided by the Holy Spirit)?

If yes, how has this impacted on your overall spiritual progress so far?

2. Specific Resources –This could range from receiving training by experienced leaders who have a proven track record and can support/mentor you in your purpose, to reading books, journals and articles from careful online research.

Action:

List 2 examples of specific resources you have already explored.

How are you utilising and building on the knowledge you have gained?

For further help and tailored support, you can email me at **dzana@pebblesforthesoul.com** to get your personalised ***Progress Action Plan Sheet*** (PAP Sheet) – A proven invaluable resource to keep you on track with your plans and goals.

* See Pebble 4

Moving On (Part 2): Divine Gifts

This is given to you by The Holy Spirit. Examples include insight, discernment, knowledge, wisdom etc.

"Ask and it will be given to you…" (Matthew 7:7)

1. Insight

Having Insight will enable you hear, see and craft your vision, walk in your purpose accurately. Divine insight goes hand in hand with God's Word so whatever insight you receive must be prayerfully checked that it is in line with the Scriptures. The more time you make for personal devotion and Bible study, the better equipped you will be to utilise this gift of insight.

Give 2 examples of when you perceived God was leading you concerning your purpose and how you followed through with the directive.

2. Wisdom

Charles Spurgeon's famous quote on wisdom says: *"Wisdom is the right use of knowledge. To know, is not to be wise. Many men know a great deal and are all the greater fools for it. There is no fool so great a fool as a knowing fool. But to know how to use knowledge is to have wisdom."*

With wisdom, you will know what to do and what *not* to do.

Give 2 examples of how you have applied divine wisdom and the result(s) that followed.

Action:

Read 2 Peter 1:5-11 and list the ingredients needed for spiritual progress.

From the Bible passage you have just read, what assurance has been given if you apply the ingredients to your spiritual life?

Light

The entrance of Your WORD gives light.

(Psalm 119:130)

"Light is the invaluable resource that conveys God's Word which ultimately guarantees progress. Light is made available by God's grace" – *Pebbles for the Soul* ©

- Light brings spiritual illumination
- Light dispels darkness
- Light reveals the way out of darkness
- Light exposes the truth

The story of creation records that light was needed in the beginning (see Genesis 1:1-5). *When you walk in the light, you can see the way forward.

Action:

List 3 areas in your life where you need clarity.

* Use the poem **Let There be Light** as a prayer declaration (see **Appendices**).

The Secret: LIGHT

Let us look at John 1:1-5.

"In the beginning was The Word and The Word was with God and the Word Was God. He was in the beginning with God. All things were made through Him, and without Him nothing was made that was made. In Him was life, and the life was the light of men. And the light shines in the darkness, and the darkness did not comprehend it."

This is the secret revealed if you can grasp it: The Word of God is Jesus, and He is THE LIGHT. When you give Him permission to operate in your life, you will not stumble in the darkness of ignorance.

It takes the following to access Light:

Brokenness (laying down of self, realising your life belongs to God).

Humility (acknowledging the need for God and others, embracing truth about who you are in Christ) Remember, God resists the proud but gives grace to the humble (1 Peter 5:5).

Actions:

Think about areas in your life where you are yet to allow God to take charge. Remember Jesus (Word, Light) came to give abundant life, but you need to let go of your own ways and in humility, accept to follow His Way.

List 3 practical ways you will allow the LIGHT of God's Word into your heart, that will enable you to enable you to hear and see more clearly.

How to Walk in the Light of GOD

1. Surrender your agenda and your ego cravings.

"An inflated ego narrows our vision, corrupts our behaviour. When we believe we are the sole architects of our success, we tend to be ruder, more selfish and more likely to interrupt others. This is especially true in the face of setbacks and criticism. In this way, an inflated ego prevents us from learning from our mistakes and creates a defensive wall that makes it difficult to appreciate the rich lessons we glean from failure." – (Source: *Harvard Business Review: 'Ego is the Enemy of Good Leadership'*)

2. Put God first. Love Him with all your heart, soul and mind. (Matthew 22:37)

3. Choose to align your life with God's Word daily.

The phrase '*What Would Jesus Do?*" was a very popular reminder for Christians in the 1990s and in my opinion, a timeless phrase. The phrase became popular from the book *In His Steps: What Would Jesus Do* by Charles Sheldon. Wristbands were also printed with WWJD as an accessory designed for Christian youth and adults to help them remember to choose Jesus' way daily.

Can you briefly list and explain 2 other ways of walking in the light of God?

Finally, when God's light gains entrance into your soul, you are empowered by the Holy Spirit. God's light brings His specific Word regarding your circumstances, His promises, plans and purpose for you. This takes you to your next level of spiritual progress.

You are empowered to:

1. **Arise**: Wake up from the place where life and its 'lemons' (aka challenging circumstances) have kept you.

2. **Shine**: Show up to the world and be radiant with the glory of The Lord. Everything and everyone was created to reflect GLORY! (See Isaiah 60:1)

Declaration of Commitment

Heavenly Father, according to Your Word in 1 Timothy 4:15, I commit to making the time to actively meditate on Your Word and engage with the grace You have given for my spiritual journey to wholeness in spirit, soul, and body so that my progress will be evident to all. I take responsibility for my spiritual progress, and I ask for Your help in achieving this in Jesus' Name.

> Meditate on these things; give yourself entirely to them, that your progress may be evident to all.
>
> (1 Timothy 4:15)

What others are saying…

I really, really LOVE your Blog, the inspiring words, the simple but authentic messages and everything. God bless your efforts and continue to let your flame burn ever bright. You are a beacon of hope and positivity. Bless you for that and more.

K Korgba

Pebble 7: Transformation

From Day 7: Change your mind
- The power of a transformed mind, experiencing continuous growth and change.

And do not be conformed to this world, but be transformed by the renewing of your mind that you may prove what is that good and acceptable and perfect will of God.

(Romans 12:2)

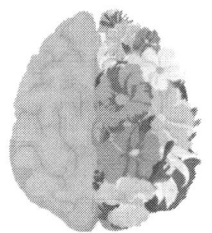

Renewing Your Mind

The invisible chains of deception, lack of encouragement and rejection are some of the shackles that having the mind of Christ is able to break- **completely**. The reason Jesus came to earth is to set the captives free! (See Isaiah 61:1)

List 5 areas in your life where you have experienced freedom from mental strongholds:

How are you maintaining a healthy mindset – daily, weekly, and monthly?

More About the Mind

Your mind is spiritual. It is your interface between the spirit realm and the physical realm. Winning victory in the battle of the mind is the first step to hosting a powerful gateway for the will, good plans and purposes of God to be revealed and birthed in the physical realm.

Here are 4 strategies that can help you to win the victory in the battle of the mind:

1. Prayer
2. The whole armour of God (Ephesians 6:11-18)
3. Praise & Worship
4. Taking Communion
5. Thanksgiving/Gratitude

Can you list 2 more?

How do you put into practice the 2 strategies you listed?

Seeing as God Sees

Cast your mind back to a time where you overcame a mental stronghold.

Use the space below to record your experience and the steps you took to gain victory (include how long it took you, how the experience positively changed your perspective, and any other areas that come to mind).

The Ministry of The Holy Spirit

1 Corinthians 2:9-11 says:

Eye has not seen, nor ear heard, nor have entered into the heart of man the things which God has prepared for those who love Him. But God has revealed them to us through His Spirit. For the Spirit searches all things, yes, the deep things of God.

The Holy Spirit is given the opportunity to function through a transformed mind by bringing revelation of deep mysteries and hidden truths which we need for life and godliness. Our success in the life here and now depends on the *wisdom, knowledge* and *understanding* of God's will for us.

List *seven other benefits* of operating with a transformed mind.

The Growth Mindset

Dr Carol Dweck explains in her book 'Mindset' The new Psychology of Success:

"Even in the growth mindset, failure can be a painful experience. But it doesn't define you. It's a problem to be faced, dealt with and learned from". A growth mindset thrives on challenge and sees failure "not as evidence of unintelligence but as a heartening springboard for growth and for stretching our existing abilities."

The challenges we face in life are opportunities for growth, personal development and resilience. They ultimately contribute to shaping who we become.

Transformation could be defined as a change or alteration especially a radical one. Having a growth mindset keeps you on track along the journey of achieving purpose and destiny.

5 ways to develop a growth mindset:

- Acknowledge and embrace imperfections
- Value the *process* over the end result
- Cultivate a sense of purpose
- Stop seeking approval
- Learn from other people's mistakes

Saga Briggs – InformED Article on 25 Ways to develop a growth mindset

Can you list 5 more?

Pebble 8: Authentic Living

From Day 8: New Day

- New beginning, maintaining wholeness in spirit, soul and body, maintaining a lifestyle of growth, community, alignment.

> Therefore, if anyone is in Christ, he is a new creation; old things have passed away; behold, all things have become new.
>
> (2 Corinthians 5:17)

New Day New You

Therefore, if anyone is in Christ, he is a new creation; old things have passed away; behold, all things have become new. (2 Corinthians 5:17)

Now you know the truth and the knowledge has set you free. You need to walk in the consciousness of the truth about who you are – In Christ. The old has gone, the new is here and you have woken up so to speak, into this New Day of realisation.

You have been given permission by God to live out your TRUE SELF – in other words, live authentically as God originally intended.

What does this look like?

You have been set free, and you are ready to flourish. This will involve ongoing commitment to:

- Developing your potential
- Seeking authenticity and excellence
- Taking responsibility for your personal growth
- Being open to new opportunities
- Expressing gratitude
- Learning to love your neighbour as yourself

Briefly describe how you intend to commit to each of the above areas. Can you list 5 more areas you can commit to?

Daily Strategies to Help You Live Authentically

- Become more aware of what is going on in your body
- Listen to your inner voice rather than losing it in the noise of others (this way you can hear, focus and visualise your hopes, dreams and goals better)
- Know yourself – your strengths, weaknesses, etc. Being honest is a powerful virtue that can release you into freedom
- Set clear boundaries
- Take time to de-clutter certain areas in your life
- Wake up every day, and be intentional about being you
- Make informed choices and take responsibility for the choices you make
- Daily Bible based declarations using 'I am…'
- Forgive
- Forbear
- Laugh more

What others are saying…

I met with Dzana during the pandemic. She is polite approachable, punctual, reliable, welcoming and friendly with a heart of gold. Dzana has a wealth of experience from studying law to working with young people alongside life coaching skills.

Thank you for helping me when I thought I was a failure after suffering silent abuse at the hands of an employer. You uplifted me from feeling useless, depressed and emotionally stressed, and helped me feel my worth and believe in myself again. Thank you for giving me a voice and helping me take control of my life one step at a time.

I would recommend Dzana to anyone who needs to change direction or create a work-life balance. She is always striving to learn more.

S Vaghela

You've Got to Pray

Prayer is one key strategy to utilise daily that will help you evolve into superior versions of who you are as you continue to live authentically. It is a two-way communication between you and God.

An example is seen when Jesus prayed (Luke 9:29): *"As He prayed, the appearance of His face was altered, and His robe became white and glistening."*

Prayer helps to remove layers of falsehood and guides you into all truth.

Prayer, guided by the Holy Spirit and God's Word, brings you into alignment with God's perfect will for you as Romans 8:26–27 reveals:

"Likewise, the Spirit also helps in our weaknesses. For we do not know what we should pray for as we ought, but the Spirit Himself makes intercession for us with groanings which cannot be uttered. Now He who searches the hearts knows what the mind of the Spirit is, because He makes intercession for the saints according to the will of God."

***Actions*:**

1. Pray and ask God to help you know His will for your life today. You can write your prayer in the space below.

In the lyrics from the song titled: *'Pray'* by MC Hammer from his third album *'Please Hammer don't hurt 'em'* (1990), Hammer recognises the importance of prayer to achieve great success in purpose and destiny.

Authentic living involves a balance between what is occurring within us and how we express and represent ourselves outside. It requires us to remove many of the defence mechanisms that have formed in childhood to protect us. (Jeremy Sutton, article on *Authentic Living,* Positive Psychology.com).

2. List 3 defence mechanisms you feel have formed in your life right from childhood, that have prevented you from connecting positively with those around you.

Owe No One Anything

Owe no one anything except to love one another, for he who loves another has fulfilled the law. (Romans 13:8)

With reference to defence mechanisms you mentioned, and as the popular saying goes, "No man is an island". We were designed for community and connection to help us thrive and flourish. This calls for the need to be vulnerable (open) so we can accommodate those around us and help us develop valuable relationships.

Pause here and ask yourself: "*How comfortable am I with admitting my mistakes?*"

Describe how you feel when you know you need to own up to your actions towards someone you have offended.

In what ways can you show vulnerability to those around you, without compromising on being yourself?

Brené Brown in her book titled: *Daring Greatly: How the Courage to Be Vulnerable Transforms The Way We Live, Love, Parent and Lead*, reinforces the strong connection between authenticity and vulnerability, She states: "Vulnerability is the birthplace of love, belonging, joy, courage, empathy and creativity. It is the source of hope, empathy, accountability, and authenticity."

List 2 ways you can express vulnerability to those around you for each of the following:

Love:

Courage:

Empathy:

The security you experience coming from the depth of God's love and knowing that He accepts you settles any doubts about your significance and what treasures you have been blessed with to share with the world.

Do you agree/disagree with the above statement? If yes or no, why?

Finally…

Authentic living is about having a settled, unshakeable confidence in who you are, and living *from* that consciousness. You are better positioned to achieve great success from that realm of living and this is connected to the ABUNDANT LIFE Jesus Christ brings.

Action:

List 7 positive habits you will commit to learn which will help you achieve great success and maintain authentic living.

CONGRATULATIONS! You have completed all 8 Pebbles. WELLDONE!

I would love to read your feedback on how this book, "**When I found YOU, I found Me**", and the 8 Pebbles companion guide have helped you in navigating your path to maintaining a healthy soul and achieving purpose. Feel free to also email me specific areas you would like further help and guidance with at **dzana@pebblesforthesoul.com**

For more resources, keep an eye out for my upcoming book titled **Just For You Today** which is a collection of 40 powerful inspirational quotes to help you on your journey in authentic living.

Please share this book's ISBN with your contacts to help empower and transform their lives for good!

Black and White interior ISBN: 9798356425523

Wishing your continued success.

Thank you!

Dzana

About The Author

Dzana is passionate about growth, mentoring and bringing out the best in people, encouraging individuals to live out their full potential and experience the benefits of total wholeness in spirit, soul and body. She achieves this through her transformational Life Coaching sessions, Inspirational quotes' collections, and seasonal online book clubs aka **ReadToYOU** for both adults and children to help inspire, motivate and challenge personal growth.

Over the last decade, Dzana has been involved in shaping the next generation of leaders through mentoring children and young people with programmes creatively designed to help them discover who they are, and empowering their gifts and talents, as originally designed by God. These include workshops to inspire, motivate and support them in achieving their goals, recognising the truth that God loves them the way they are. They also provide life strategies on how to achieve positive relationships, emotional and spiritual well-being even in the stressful and challenging situations we all face throughout life. A youth leader in her local Church, Dzana has received recognition for her contribution and investment in the lives of youth.

The author has worked in multicultural and international organizations committed to making a positive difference in the lives of children, vulnerable adults, families and the environment. This has accorded her the advantage and opportunity to interact with people from all walks of life, understand people, provide guidance, strategies and insights, to help those in her sphere of influence navigate through life and find purpose. Currently living in the United Kingdom, she continues to develop her coaching and mentoring expertise alongside her role as a lawyer specializing in Immigration, Employment Law and Compliance.

A writer, jazz-lover and poet, the author has performed Spoken Word poetry and published poetry. One of her poems, **God Loves You Just the Way You Are**' was featured in a collection of hope-filled messages and poems by **Blue Mountain Arts**. Dzana has published several articles on life lessons and short stories in Law magazines with her personal column titled '**Time Out on Things Not Legal**'.

Dzana is married to the love of her life, Emmanuel and they are blessed with two A-mazing boys (Adriel & Azariah). She enjoys adventure, travelling and speaks English, Nupe, Hausa and French.

Visit Dzana on the web at: **https://dzanamadagu.com/**

Follow her on Instagram at: **@dzanamadagu**

Email the author at **dzana@pebblesforthesoul.com**

Appendices

Appendix 1. Poem

Let There Be Light

When You light the way
Then I can see
The path to take
So easily.
Let there be light
Let there be light.

It all begins with Your Word
My lamp for life
My battle sword
Let there be light
Let there be light.

Illuminate my heart
Invigorate my soul
There's power in Your light
Yes, there's power in Your light
Heaven, release light
Let there be light
Let there be light.

By Dzana Madagu

Appendix 2. Doing Life with Family

References

Pebble 1:

Cambridge Academic Content Dictionary, *Cambridge University Press,* 2022 (definition of Truth)

http://www.cbn.com/spirituallife/onlinediscipleship/easter/what_is_truth.aspx

Walter A. Elwell (ed.): *Bakers Evangelical Dictionary of Biblical Theology* 1996 Published by Baker Books, a division of Baker Book House Company, PO Box 6287, Grand rapids Michigan 49516-6287 (definition of Truth)

Pebble 2:

Cambridge Academic Content Dictionary, *Cambridge University Press,* 2022, (definition of Freedom)

Pebble 3:

Developinggoodhabits.com

Dr Cindy Trimm: 'Reclaim Your Soul' Your Journey to Personal Empowerment, 2014.

Pebble 4:

Collins COBUILD *Advanced Learner's Dictionary* (definition of Empower)

Dictionary.com (definition of Growth)

Dr Jacqueline N Samuels: *Push Through: Release Your Past and Step into Your Divine Destiny,* 2018.

Investors in People.com

James Clear: *Atomic Habits: An Easy and Proven Way to Build Good Habits & Break Bad Ones,* 2018.

John C Maxwell: The15 Invaluable *Laws of Growth: Live Them and Reach Your Potential,* 2012.

MindTools.com

Pebble 5:

Cambridge Academic Content Dictionary, *Cambridge University Press* 2022 (definition of clarity)

Dr Cindy Trimm: *'Hello, TOMORROW!' The Transformational Power of Vision,* 2018.

Roy T Bennett: *The Light in the Heart*, 2016.

Pebble 6:

Charles Sheldon: *In His Steps: What Would Jesus Do. Originally published in 1897*

Harvard Business Review: *'Ego is the Enemy of Good Leadership'* by Rasmus Hougaard and Jacqueline Carter November 06, 2018.

Pebble 7:

Dr Carol Dweck: *'Mindset' The New Psychology of Success,* 2016.

Saga Briggs: InformED Article on *25 Ways to develop a growth mindset*. February 10, 2015.

Pebble 8:

Brené Brown: *Daring Greatly: How the Courage to Be Vulnerable Transforms The Way We Live, Love, Parent and Lead,* 2015.

Jeremy Sutton: *Authentic Living: How to be Real According to Psychology 10 March 2021. Positive Psychology.com*

MC Hammer: 'Pray' from *'Please Hammer don't hurt 'em'* album, 1990.

Printed in Great Britain
by Amazon